Vedic Astrology

A Beginner's Guide to the Fundamentals of Jyotish and Hindu Astrology

By: Discover Press

Table of Contents

Introduction 1

Chapter One: What Is Vedic Astrology? 3

    The Background and Origin of Vedic Astrology 3

    Western vs. Vedic Astrology 4

    How Is Vedic Astrology Used? 10

Chapter Two: The Zodiac Signs 18

    Aries (Mesha): April 14 - May 14 18

    Taurus (Vrisha): May 15 - June 14 19

    Gemini (Mithuna): June 15 - July 14 20

    Cancer (Karka): July 15 - August 16 21

    Leo (Simha): August 16 - September 15 22

    Virgo (Kanya): September 16 - October 16 23

    Libra (Tula): October 17 - November 14 24

    Scorpio (Vrishchika): November 15 - December 15 25

    Sagittarius (Dhanu): December 16 - January 13 26

    Capricorn (Makara): January 14 - February 13 27

    Aquarius (Kumbha): February 14 - March 14 28

    Pisces (Meena): March 15 - April 15 29

Chapter Three: The Elements (Tattvas) 31

    Fire (Agni) 32

    Earth (Prithvi) 37

    Air (Vayu) 42

Water (Jal) 48

Space (Akasa) 52

Chapter Four: The Planets (Navagrahas) **54**

Chapter Five: The Lunar Mansions (Nakshatras) **62**

Chapter Six: The Houses (Bhavas) **79**

Chapter Seven: Reading a Vedic Birth Chart (Kundli) **89**

How to Read Your Vedic Kundli 91

Conclusion **96**

Introduction

If you want to learn more about Vedic astrology, then you must be wondering what the stars have to tell you about your life. Maybe you are looking for answers as to why the same patterns keep repeating themselves in your life, or maybe you are seeking an explanation for why some people seem to be born under a lucky star, while others are destined for suffering and misfortune.

Vedic astrology can offer explanations for these things and much, much more. According to Vedic astrology, all of the incidents that occur in your life and everything about your character is determined by the placement of the planets at the time of your birth. People have been using Vedic astrology for countless years to predict personality traits, career paths, marriages, and more. It explains your karma, what you may have experienced in past lives, and why you may be reaping the benefits or paying debts from another lifetime.

Learning the concepts of Vedic astrology and understanding the significance of your birth chart can help you understand why you are the way you are in the present, why you have had the experiences of your past, and what you are destined for in the future. It can help put your strengths and weaknesses into focus as well as let go of paths that you have been holding onto that will only lead to dead ends.

Vedic astrology can help you heal your romantic relationships and friendships, boost your career, improve your health, and derive more joy from living day to day life. The more you open up your mind, develop your intuition, and learn about the concepts of Vedic astrology, the more you will be able to understand the deeper meaning of your life and find your purpose.

This book includes everything you need to know about the basics of Vedic astrology, including:

- What Vedic astrology is and how it differs from Western astrology
- What the different zodiac signs are and their meanings
- The natural elements and their significance
- The planets and their importance on the birth chart
- The house and lunar mansions and what they signify
- How to read the basics on a Vedic birth chart

And much, much more!

Vedic astrology tells you that your destiny was written in the stars at your time of birth, and it even led you to this very moment of reading this text. So, what are you waiting for? Keep reading to find out the secrets of the universe and unlock your full potential.

Chapter One: What Is Vedic Astrology?

The Background and Origin of Vedic Astrology

Vedic astrology, also known as Hindu, Indian, or Jyotisha/Jyotishya astrology, is the Hindu version of astrology. The terms Vedic, Hindu, Indian, and Jyotisha astrology can be used interchangeably. Jyotisha comes from the word Jyotish, which means light. The term Jyotisha refers to the study of astrology, astronomy, and the science of keeping time according to the movements of heavenly bodies. Jyotisha is used to maintain the calendar, keep time, and predict auspicious timing for rituals and events.

Although Vedic astrology is based on the scientific movements and locations of celestial bodies, it is important to note that Vedic astrology is technically classified as a pseudoscience. All forms of astrology have been rejected by the scientific community, as there have been scientific tests on astrology that haven't provided any evidence supporting the system.

While it does not qualify as a science, Vedic astrology also does not fit into the category of religion. This allows many Indian universities to offer advanced degrees in the study of astrology. There is also a widespread movement to include astrology with other related teachings, such as yoga and tantra.

Simply put, Vedic astrology is the science and study of light and the multitude of ways that the heavenly bodies affect earthly beings.

Western vs. Vedic Astrology

Depending on where you're from, you might be more familiar with the principles and teachings of Western astrology than Vedic astrology. While Western astrology is the more traditional form of astrology in the western hemisphere, Vedic astrology is more popular in the east. The two are actually quite similar, but with some important distinctions.

Calendar

One of the most significant differences between Western and Vedic astrology is the calendar each practice uses. Since so much of astrology is based on the calendar, this is a critical distinction that changes many layers of both versions of astrology.

Western astrology uses the tropical calendar, which is a fixed system that defines the year and therefore the dates of each of the astrological signs. Vedic astrology uses the sidereal system, which uses corrective systems called ayanamsas to account for the precession of equinoxes.

This means that while the order of the signs for both astrology systems remains the same, the dates correlated with each sign are different. For example, Aries is the first zodiac sign in both systems, but the dates for Aries begin on March 21st for Western astrology and April 13th for Vedic astrology.

The dates for each astrology system are as follows:

Zodiac Sign	Western Astrology	Vedic Astrology
Aries	March 21 - April 19	April 13 - May 14
Taurus	April 20 - May 20	May 15 - June 14
Gemini	May 21 - June 21	June 15 - July 14
Cancer	June 22 - July 22	July 15 - August 14
Leo	July 23 - August 22	August 15 - September 15
Virgo	August 23 - September 22	September 16 - October 15
Libra	September 23 - October 23	October 16 - November 14
Scorpio	October 24 - November 22	November 15 - December 14
Sagittarius	November 23 - December 21	December 15 - January 13
Capricorn	December 22 - January 19	January 14 - February 11
Aquarius	January 20 - February 18	February 12 - March 12
Pisces	February 19 - March 20	March 13 - April 12

As you can see, the subtle shift in dates completely changes when the signs begin and end for each version of astrology.

The reason for this shift is that Vedic astrology uses corrective math to adjust the signs as the positions of the planets change. Tropical and sidereal systems have moved away from one another at a rate of about one degree every 72 years. There is currently approximately a 24-degree difference between the two systems.

Although there is no "right" or "wrong" version of astrology, and one system is no better than the other, Vedic astrology may be considered more accurate since it accounts for the changing planetary positions.

Karma and Personality

Both Vedic and Western astrology are used to select auspicious timings for events. Vedic astrology predicts more specifically the events in a person's life, such as when they will get married or even the exact time of death.

Vedic astrology focuses more on an individual's past, present, and future karma, while Western astrology is used more to predict a person's personality and motivations.

Planets

Another big difference between Western and Vedic astrology is their use of the planets. Vedic astrology focuses solely on celestial bodies that are visible to the naked eye.

These planets include Mercury, Venus, Mars, Jupiter, Saturn, the Sun, and the Moon.

Western astrology not only uses the heavenly bodies we can see, but also the planets and asteroids that are only visible from Earth by using a telescope. Western astrology uses the same planets as Vedic astrology and additionally includes Uranus, Neptune, Pluto, and more.

Besides the visible planets, Vedic astrology also uses the two lunar nodes (referred to as Rahu and Ketu). Western astrology uses the two nodes, but they aren't named the same way, nor do they hold the same significance as they do in Vedic astrology.

Not only do the two systems use different heavenly bodies, but they also have divergent perspectives on the strength and weakness of the planets. A retrograde is a period when a planet appears, from Earth, to spin backward in its orbit. This is merely an optical illusion, as the planet isn't actually moving backward. Astronomers refer to this phenomenon as "apparent retrograde motion."

In Western astrology, planets in retrograde are viewed as weakened. The most popular and well-known example of this is Mercury retrograde. Mercury has a retrograde period about three to four times each year, lasting approximately three weeks each period. Mercury is the planet of communication. So, according to Western astrology, when Mercury is in retrograde, all areas of life surrounding communication move backward instead of forward. This means that disagreements, scheduling problems, miscommunications, technology struggles, and accidents are believed to occur much more frequently during this period.

Vedic astrology believes the opposite about retrogrades. Remember, Vedic astrology only uses the celestial bodies that are visible from Earth. When planets are retrograde, they appear larger, brighter and more visible to us. It makes sense that in Vedic astrology, this means that planets in retrograde are actually considered stronger.

Importance of the Signs

One great distinction between Vedic and Western astrology is the emphasis each system places on the different placements of signs on a birth chart.

In both systems, an individual has a sun/star sign, a moon sign, and a rising sign. The sun or star sign is determined by just your date of birth, while your moon and rising signs also require the exact time and location of your birth to get an accurate reading.

In Western astrology, the sun or star sign is the most significant aspect of a person's chart. The sun sign reveals how you interact with others and the world around you. This is the sign that's based solely on your date of birth, and it's the sign that most people who have a basic knowledge of Western astrology know about themselves.

The moon sign is considered the second most important aspect, and conveys your private, emotional nature and who you are when you're alone.

Vedic astrology, on the other hand, places the most emphasis on the rising sign. The rising sign is the "mask" that you wear, the first impression you make, and the way that you appear to others. The rising sign is considered much more important than the sun sign in Vedic astrology, followed by the moon sign.

Origins

Vedic astrology originates from the Vedas, which are the sacred texts of Hinduism. Many scholars consider Hinduism to be the oldest religious tradition, and today it is the third-largest religion in the world.

The Vedas, which originated in ancient India, are the oldest scriptures of Hinduism and the oldest layer of Sanskrit literature. Vedic astrology is considered to be the word of God. Although Vedic astrology uses updated mathematical calculations, it is widely seen as a more spiritual practice than Western astrology.

Unlike Vedic astrology, Western astrology originated in ancient Greece with influences from ancient Egypt as well. Rather than spirituality and religion, Western astrology is more closely related to philosophy and psychology.

Which System Should You Use?

There is no correct answer to which astrology system you should use. It is a very personal choice that only you can make for yourself. Learn as much as you can about both systems, and use your judgment and intuition to guide you towards which one works best for you.

There are many ways to choose which system you want to use, and you can create your own method. One way to decide is by observing the people closest to you. Make a list of their characteristics and compare them to the personality traits associated with both their Vedic and Western astrology signs (if they are different; there is currently some overlap between the two versions, so some birth dates are the same sign in both Vedic and Western astrology).

You may notice a pattern where people more closely align with the traits assigned to them through Vedic astrology, or perhaps they are more like their Western zodiac signs. Go with what your instincts tell you is the more accurate and frequently correct system.

How Is Vedic Astrology Used?

Although the uses of Vedic astrology have changed over the centuries since its inception, there are many modern uses for the Vedic astrology system today.

Teach Indian Culture

Vedic astrology is an important facet of Indian culture, both in the past and the present. It contains the spiritual and religious traditions of ancient India, and it keeps them alive even to this day. The mythology behind Vedic astrology is also closely tied to Indian culture.

Although it is technically classified as a pseudoscience, many people in India today accept Vedic astrology as a science and it is an integral part of their everyday lives.

Auspicious Timing

In the past, Vedic astrology was used to select the timing of religious sacrifices and rituals. While these practices have changed and evolved over time, this system is still used to predict the most auspicious timing for rituals, events, and ceremonies.

You might use Vedic astrology to determine your ideal wedding date (or predict when you will get married, for that matter). You could use it to determine when the best time is to make a business deal, or when you should avoid negotiating pay rates. Vedic astrology can predict the best times to travel, when to conceive a child, and so much more.

Naming Children

According to Vedic astrology, a child's name shapes their personality and what they will attract into their life as they grow into adulthood. Choosing the right name is an important step for parents towards setting up their child for a happy, successful future. Vedic astrology has been used to name children for centuries, and a baby's naming ceremony (widely known as Naamkaran) is a significant event for both parents and children.

Vedic astrology combines astrological aspects with numerology to determine the most prosperous name for a child based on their birth information. To find the ideal baby name, you will need all of the same information you would use to formulate a birth chart, including the date, exact time, and location of birth.

The first two letters of the name should be after the birth time Rashi. Rashi is the moon sign on a person's birth chart. The letters associated with the birth time Rashi come from the Vedas. Here are the 12 Rashis and their associated naming letters:

Aries	Chu, Che, Cho, La, Li, Lu, Le, Lo, A
Taurus	E, V, Ai, O, Vaa, Vi, Vu, Ve, Vo
Gemini	Ka, Ki, Ku, Gh, Chh, Ke, Ko, Ha
Cancer	Hi, Hu, He, Ho, Da, Di, Du, De, Do
Leo	M, Mi, Mu, Me, Mo, Ta, Ti, Tu, Te
Virgo	To, Pa, Pi, Pe, Sha, Thha, Pe, Po
Libra	Ra, Ri, Ru, Re, Ro, Taa, Ti, Tu, Te
Scorpio	To, N, Ni, Nu, Ne, No, Ya, Yi, Yu
Sagittarius	Ye, Yo, Bha, Bhi, Bhu, Dha, Pha (F), Dhha, Bhe
Capricorn	Bho, Ja, Ji, Khi, Khu, Khe, Kho, Ga, Gi
Aquarius	Gu, Ge, Go, Sa, Si, Soo, Se, So, Da
Pisces	Di, Du, Thha, Jha, Jya, De, Do, Ch, Chi

As you can see, there are multiple options for the first two letters for each Rashi. So, for example, a child with a Rashi or moon in Aries should have a first name starting with the letters La, Le, or Li. Some Rashi share letters with other Rashi (e.g.: both Leo and Libra have Ti, Tu, and Te listed as options). This means that a child born with a Rashi or moon in Leo could have the same first two letters in their name as a child born with a Rashi or moon in Libra.

After finding the options for the first two letters using the child's Rashi, the next step is to use numerology to select the best, luckiest letters. Each letter of the alphabet correlates with a single-digit number as follows:

1	A, I, J, Q, Y
2	B, K, R
3	C, G, L, S
4	O, M, T
5	E, H, N, X
6	U, V, W
7	O, Z
8	F, P

You can determine a child's single-digit Birth Number, also called a Life Path Number or Ruling Number, by adding the numbers of a child's birthdate and reducing them to a single digit.

For example, for a child born on April 17, 1990, or 04/17/1990, you would calculate the Birth Number as follows:

04 + 17 + 1990 = 2011

2 + 0 + 1 + 1 = 4

You can also calculate the Birth Number by separating each digit in the birth date and adding them as follows:

0 + 4 + 1 + 7 + 1 + 9 + 9 + 0 = 31

3 + 1 = 4

As you can see, you will get the same result regardless of which method you use.

Once you have calculated the Birth Number down to a single digit, you find the letters associated with that number on the chart above. Use any of these letters (or a combination of these letters) in the child's name. Using more than one letter or any letter more than once is extra lucky.

But the Birth Number does not only tell you which letters you should include when naming your baby. It also tells you which letters to avoid.

You should not use letters associated with certain numbers due to the relationship between the numbers.

The numbers 1, 2, 4, and 7 get along with each other. So, if your child's Birth Number is 4, you should definitely use the letters associated with 4, and you can also safely use the letters associated with 1, 2, and 7.

The numbers 6 and 8 do not get along with 1, 2, 4, and 7, so you should avoid using any of the letters associated with 6 and 8 in your child's name.

The reverse is also true: if your child's Birth Number is 6, you should strive to use only letters associated with 6 and 8, and avoid letters associated with 1, 2, 4, and 7.

The number 5 is considered neutral and can be used safely in combination with any other Birth Number.

In Vedic astrology, the parents' names are also significant in naming a child, especially if the parents were named using the system outlined above. It is common practice to use the first letter of a parent's name as the first letter of the child's name, particularly if the letters associated with the parent's and child's Rashi are the same.

For example, if both the parent and the child have Libra as their moon sign or Rashi, using the letters associated with the Libra Rashi are the luckiest. If the parent has a Leo moon sign/Rashi and the child has a Libra moon sign/Rashi, then the letters those two moon signs have in common are Ti, Tu, and Te. It would be most lucky for the child to choose a name starting with these letters because it both follows the Rashi naming chart and connects to the parent's name and Rashi.

After doing so many calculations to find the luckiest name for your baby, you don't have to come up with a unique name. You can choose from a list of popular names and just make sure that the name fits with your calculations. This is much easier than trying to come up with a brand new name that meets all of the qualifications for a prosperous name according to Vedic astrology and numerology. In the modern world, there are many calculators online that can help Vedic astrologers easily find a list of name suggestions based on a child's date of birth.

If you want to choose a name for yourself or a child based on Vedic astrology, you can skip these manual calculations by using a generator from a reputable online source.

Matchmaking (Kundli)

Kundali matching, or Kundli, is the term for matchmaking based on the Vedic astrology system. In ancient Indian tradition, Vedic astrology was used to predict the compatibility between a man and a woman for arranged marriages. This would not only help determine how well their personalities would get along with each other but also their chances of having children and a successful life together.

Many people still use Vedic astrology to this day to predict romantic compatibility. By comparing the birth charts of two people, you will get a clear picture of what their relationship would be like and whether they are destined for success or failure as a couple.

Much like the process of naming children, there are many generators online today that can be used to predict the marriage compatibility between two people. You will need the birth information, including the date, precise time, and location, of both partners to get the most accurate prediction.

Kundli matching is not only used to find the best match but also to predict any struggles the pair may endure as a married couple. Vedic astrology also offers solutions to these potential problems, and they are tailored specifically to the needs of the two individuals.

Chapter Two: The Zodiac Signs

In Vedic astrology, there are twelve zodiac signs, and each one is named after a particular constellation. The signs have unique characteristics and personality traits that correlate with the symbolism and lore of their constellations.

These are the twelve signs of the zodiac in order, along with the basic information of each sign:

Aries (Mesha): April 14 - May 14

Element: Fire
Modality: Cardinal
Polarity: Masculine/Positive

Aries is the first sign of the zodiac, making it the youngest and most childlike sign. Aries may be innocent and naive, but they are also tough and robust.

Aries is the sign that represents the self. Aries individuals may get a bad reputation for being selfish because they are inclined to put themselves first. They are headstrong, enthusiastic, and energetic.

As a fire sign, Aries is temperamental, passionate, and vibrant. Fire signs are forceful and headstrong, and Aries is perhaps the most strong-willed of them all.

Cardinal signs are natural-born leaders, and combined with being the first sign of the zodiac, Aries is the most dominant leader of them all. They are creative and innovative, and they have a hard time respecting authority figures. They perform best when they are self-employed or in a high-ranking managerial position at their jobs because they prefer to be the one giving orders rather than taking them.

Aries is a masculine or positive sign, giving these individuals a cheerful and optimistic disposition. Aries people tend to have more stereotypically masculine qualities, such as assertiveness, strength, confidence, and courage.

Taurus (Vrisha): May 15 - June 14

Element: Earth
Modality: Fixed
Polarity: Feminine/Negative

Taurus is the second sign of the zodiac in Vedic astrology. Like its predecessor Aries, Taurus is another young and childlike sign.

But that is where the similarities between Taurus and Aries end. Despite being located directly next to one another in the zodiac, these two signs could not be more different.

Taurus is the sign of work, money, and routine. Taureans are creatures of habit and like to follow their daily routines.

Taurus is an earth sign, and earth signs are reliable and steadfast. Since Taurus is also the sign of work, typical Taureans have a remarkably strong work ethic. They don't consider any job too lowly or beneath them, and they value putting in a hard day's work to earn their money.

As a fixed sign and the sign of habits and routines, Taureans are inflexible and do not adjust well to change. They like to have thorough plans and never do anything without conducting careful research and weighing all of their options first.

Taurus is perhaps the most stubborn sign of the entire zodiac. They are unwavering in their beliefs and unyielding in their stances. Once a Taurus has made up their mind about something, nothing can change it.

As a feminine or negative sign, Taureans tend to have a pessimistic outlook on life. They are judgmental and see the flaws in a situation or a person not because they want to criticize but because they want to help. Their femininity makes them accommodating, supportive, gentle, and warm.

Gemini (Mithuna): June 15 - July 14

Element: Air
Modality: Mutable
Polarity: Masculine/Positive

Gemini is the third astrological sign, so it is still one of the youngest and most spiritually immature signs. Geminis see the world with childlike awe and wonder, and they are naturally curious about their surroundings.

Gemini is the sign of the mind, thinking, communication, and social interaction. Geminis are almost always extroverts, so they gain energy from being surrounded by other people and they need social interaction to be happy.

As a mutable sign, Geminis are adaptable and adjust easily to change. Not only does change come easily to them but they also embrace it. They look forward to trying new things and they love having new experiences.

Gemini is one of the masculine or positive signs, meaning that Geminis have typically masculine traits such as assertiveness and dominance. They are also optimistic and tend to view the glass as half-full rather than half-empty.

Cancer (Karka): July 15 - August 16

Element: Water
Modality: Cardinal
Polarity: Feminine/Negative

Cancer is the fourth sign in Vedic astrology and the last of the young, childish signs. Cancer is a very emotional sign, and combined with its childish nature, Cancers have trouble keeping their emotional reactions under control.

As a water sign, Cancers are sensitive, emotional, and intuitive. But their childish lack of self-regulation means that they can be quite moody and temperamental, swinging wildly from one emotion to the next.

On the other hand, Cancers' sensitivity also makes them quite attentive to the emotional needs of others. They are so intuitive that they can sense how others are feeling without them having to say a word.

Cancer is a cardinal sign, so Cancers are natural leaders. Since Cancer is such a creative sign, the cardinal aspect makes them especially inventive and innovative.

Cancer is a feminine or negative sign, so Cancers portray a lot of stereotypically feminine traits. They are prone to anxiety and depression because of their innately pessimistic worldview.

Leo (Simha): August 16 - September 15

Element: Fire
Modality: Fixed
Polarity: Masculine/Positive

Leo is the fifth sign of the zodiac and marks the beginning of more spiritually mature signs. If the fire sign Aries is an infant, then the next fire sign, Leo, is an adolescent or young adult.

As a fire sign, Leo is passionate, energetic, and enthusiastic. Leos enjoy attention and are very proud. Since they live for praise and admiration, a Leo is likely to have a career as a performer or entertainer. They are also quite expressive and never hold back their feelings. Many Leos are professional actors/actresses, musicians, singers, comedians, or dancers.

As a fixed sign, Leos are quite stubborn and set in their ways. They aren't interested in trying new ways of doing things and they adjust slowly to progress and change.

Since Leo is a masculine or positive sign, all Leos, including Leo women, tend to portray some of the stereotypically male characteristics like leadership and independence. They can also be a bit irresponsible and insensitive.

Virgo (Kanya): September 16 - October 16

Element: Earth
Modality: Mutable
Polarity: Negative/Feminine

Like Leo, Virgo is spiritually one of the adolescent or young adult signs. While younger signs are primarily interested in themselves and exploring the world around them, young adult signs are more concerned with other people and their relationships with them.

Earth sign Virgo values stability and consistency. Virgo is a very honest sign, sometimes to a fault. They are fixers by nature, so they are always looking for the flaws and imperfections in people and situations. They seek to improve people and help make them better, not hurt them; but sometimes their brutal honesty comes off as harsh and cruel rather than helpful.

Mutable signs are adaptable and versatile, which tells us that mutable sign Virgo is accommodating and adjusts well to change. They don't need to take charge, but they will go along with what others want and they aren't as stubborn as many other signs.

With a negative or feminine polarity, a Virgo has a generally pessimistic disposition that is in keeping with their nature as a fixer. They also portray some of the typically feminine traits, such as nurturing, supportiveness, and sweetness.

Libra (Tula): October 17 - November 14

Element: Air
Modality: Cardinal
Polarity: Masculine/Positive

Libra is among the spiritually adolescent or young adult signs of the zodiac, meaning that Librans are primarily concerned with their interpersonal relationships and how others view them. They are trying to find their role in society and their place in the world.

Air signs are social, analytical, and indecisive. Although they are kind, considerate, and generally loving, Librans think with their heads instead of their hearts. They are the social butterflies of the zodiac and are the happiest when surrounded by good friends or new people to meet. They can be a bit flaky and unreliable, and they have a hard time making any decisions.

As a cardinal sign, Librans are natural leaders and they like to take charge. While they are team players and work well with others, they have no problem taking the initiative and stepping up when no one else will. They attack problems directly instead of trying to negotiate or work around them.

As a masculine or positive sign, a Libra has a generally cheerful disposition and a sunny outlook on life. Libras also possess many stereotypically masculine qualities, such as strength, courage, and independence. They can also be imprudent and a bit rebellious.

Scorpio (Vrishchika): November 15 - December 15

Element: Water
Modality: Fixed
Polarity: Feminine/Negative

Scorpio is the last of the spiritually adolescent or young adult signs. Their spiritual age tells us that Scorpios are focused on how they present themselves to others and how they interact with the world.

As a water sign, Scorpios are powerful, mysterious, and magnetic. They are deeply emotional and sensitive, and they experience their feelings more profoundly than most. Scorpios are quite intuitive and are not only very self-aware, but can also sense the feelings and thoughts of others.

Fixed signs are very stubborn, and Scorpio is perhaps one of the most stubborn of all the zodiac signs. They must have control and they are very set in their habits and routines. They dislike change or being told what to do.

Scorpios portray several of the typically feminine traits, such as being in touch with their feelings and sensitive to their surroundings. As a negative sign, they tend to be a bit pessimistic and focus on the dark side of things. However, a Scorpio embraces the darkness and finds the beauty in it.

Sagittarius (Dhanu): December 16 - January 13

Element: Fire
Modality: Mutable
Polarity: Masculine/Positive

Sagittarius is the first of the oldest signs of the zodiac in Vedic astrology. As a more spiritually mature sign, others may refer to Sagittarius individuals as "old souls." Sagittarians are carefree in a way that suggests that they've seen it all before, have already learned plenty of hard lessons, and are now here on this earth to have fun and enjoy themselves.

Fire sign Sagittarius is feisty, impulsive, and fun-loving. A Sagittarian's zest for life is unparalleled, and they have an innate thirst for adventure and wanderlust.

As a mutable sign, Sagittarians are generally easy-going and laid-back. They can adapt well to any new environment and they enjoy meeting new people. They are happy to let others take authority and leadership roles while they fall in line and follow directions.

Sagittarius is a masculine or positive sign, which tells us that Sagittarians are eternally hopeful and optimistic. They are incredibly resilient, so they always get back up when they've been knocked down. Sagittarians have such positive attitudes that sometimes they ignore practical problems and responsibilities. They have many of the typically masculine traits, such as bravery and independence.

Capricorn (Makara): January 14 - February 13

Element: Earth
Modality: Cardinal
Polarity: Feminine/Negative

Like Sagittarius, Capricorn is another spiritually mature sign with an old soul. But instead of age bringing levity and light-heartedness to this zodiac sign, Capricorns are very serious, wise, and strict.

Earth sign Capricorn is reliable, predictable, and stable. They practice self-control in everything they do, and they are hard-working and ambitious. Capricorns are very responsible, especially when it comes to their careers and finances, and they are excellent at saving and investing money. Their greatest goal is to establish financial security for themselves, preferably through a prestigious career, and then they want to help others financially.

As a cardinal sign, Capricorns are natural-born leaders. Since their careers are so important to them, they usually take management or authority roles at work. They are also very paternal, so they tend to take the position of the "father" in any group they are in. Their friends and loved ones often turn to them for practical advice.

Capricorn is a negative or feminine sign, so they have a pessimistic worldview. They tend to complain a lot and notice the imperfections in a situation before appreciating the things that are going well.

Aquarius (Kumbha): February 14 - March 14

Element: Air
Modality: Fixed
Polarity: Masculine/Positive

Aquarius is the penultimate sign of the zodiac, making it one of the oldest and wisest souls. Aquarians possess a rare intelligence and innate wisdom that others may sense in their presence.

As an air sign, Aquarians are social, inquisitive, and analytical. While the other air signs are social in the sense that they are talkative and enjoy meeting new people, Aquarians are more humanitarian and philosophical than social. They like to observe their surroundings and study the people around them more than speaking with others directly. Aquarians are more interested in society as a whole than in individuals, and they are innovators who look for ways to make the world a better place for everyone.

Since Aquarius is a fixed sign, Aquarians are organized and stubborn. While they are innovative and inventive, they have a hard time getting new projects off the ground. Once they get started, though, they are good at seeing their goals through to the end. They are incredibly hard-headed and rebellious, so they tend to question authority and hate being told what to do. Aquarians are contrarians that will do the opposite of whatever someone directs them.

As a positive or masculine sign, Aquarians are generally hopeful and optimistic. They see the glass as half-full instead of half-empty, and while they are concerned about the state of the world and humanity, they have faith that things can change for the better.

Pisces (Meena): March 15 - April 15

Element: Water
Modality: Mutable
Polarity: Feminine/Negative

Pisces is the twelfth and final sign of the zodiac, making it spiritually the oldest and wisest of them all. Most Pisces individuals possess an other-worldly, ethereal presence, almost as if they are already finished with this life and have one foot in the next. Pisces people are largely unconcerned with reality and the world around them and instead are much more focused on the fantastical, spiritual, mythical, and abstract.

Water signs are sensitive and emotional, and no sign is more in touch with their feelings than Pisces. While they are more emotionally expressive than most other signs, they also may have a bit more emotional self-control. For example, they will cry in public not because they can't hold it in, but because they feel like they shouldn't have to. They find power in vulnerability and beauty in self-expression.

As a mutable sign, Pisces people are quite easy to get along with. They are malleable and laid-back, so they will happily go with the flow of what everyone else is doing. They are susceptible to manipulation and trickery from others because they are so agreeable and giving of themselves.

The negative polarity of a Pisces manifests not so much in a bad attitude, like most other negative signs, but in a tendency towards depression and anxiety. Pisces are also prone to excess and addiction and may struggle with mental health issues.

Chapter Three: The Elements (Tattvas)

In Vedic astrology, there are five natural elements, or Tattvas, that make up the physical world: fire (Agni), earth (Prithvi), air (Vayu), water (Jal), and space. Western astrology also connects the zodiac signs to the natural elements, but one of the key differences between Vedic and Western astrology is that Western astrology only acknowledges four elements, excluding space. Even in Vedic astrology, space differs from the other four elements because no zodiac signs are associated with space.

Each element has distinctive characteristics, and they all work together in harmony. A zodiac sign's natural element reveals a great deal about that sign's temperament and personality.

But each individual person is influenced in various amounts by all four elements. When you read any Vedic birth chart, it will include all of the houses, planets, and elements. But the position of the planets in certain houses will tell you the proportions of each element. In this way, the space element encompasses the other four elements. You will be able to predict the disposition of a person by observing how the elements are balanced on their chart.

In Ayurveda, the goal is to rebalance the elements that are out of balance in the body to achieve the best mental and physical health. In most cases, both in Ayurveda and Vedic astrology, a person is strongly influenced by two of the elements and lacks a balance of the other two forces.

Once you know which elements have the strongest presence in your chart, you will know what areas you need to work on in your life to achieve balance. It can also be interesting and informative to compare which natural elements are strongest in the Vedic astrology chart with your Ayurvedic body type.

Here are the natural elements of Vedic astrology and their defining characteristics:

Fire (Agni)

The fire element rules three signs in Vedic astrology: Aries (Mesha), Leo (Simha), and Sagittarius (Dhanus). Mars is the primary ruler of the fire signs and is the sole ruler of Aries. The Sun and Jupiter are also fiery planets but to a lesser extent, and are the guiding heavenly bodies of Leo and Sagittarius, respectively.

Characteristics

The fire element represents passion, energy, and enthusiasm. Fire is an intense motivator that drives us to succeed, conquer, and let go of the past and anything that no longer serves us. It is a destructive force, but destruction is often necessary to clear the path and make room for fresh, new growth. Fire can also be a force of evolution, since it provides warmth, heat, and light for all living things to flourish.

Individuals born under the fire signs Aries, Leo, and Sagittarius tend to be boisterous, courageous, aggressive, joyful, active, and determined. They have loud personalities and strong presences, so others tend to take note when any fire signs enter the room.

Since the element of fire is a cleanser and a conqueror, fire sign people are ambitious, self-motivated, and resilient. They stop at nothing to achieve their goals, and when obstacles block their paths or knock them down, they only grow stronger and emerge more powerful than ever.

Imbalances

In the body, the fire element is crucial to the digestive system, mental processing, and energy levels. Too much or too little fire in the body can lead to stomach problems, weight imbalances, and frantic or low energy. Mentally, fire gives us passion, determination, confidence, and the drive to succeed. An imbalance of fire in the mind can lead to impulsivity, overconfidence, egotism, bossiness, lethargy, or depression.

An imbalance of fire can affect a person's personality and disposition as well as the body. Too much fire leads to anger, aggression, violence, selfishness, fanaticism, and overindulgence. It can also cause burnout from working too hard, physical overexertion, or starting too many projects without conserving enough energy and resources to see them through to the end.

A lack of fire makes people cold, aloof, and inexpressive. They are passionless and lack ambition, enthusiasm, creativity, and physical energy. They may have a slow metabolism, dull eyes, and a weak immune system. Too little fire creates a lack of motivation and persistence to succeed or try new things.

The Signs

Aries (Mesha)

While they are all ruled by the fire element, fire manifests differently in each of the three fire signs. The fire characteristics shine through each sign in many positive and negative ways.

As the zodiac sign ruled by Mars, Aries is perhaps the best representation of a pure fire sign. The fire in Aries manifests as impulsivity, physical and emotional strength, frank honesty, and bravery.

Aries people are self-starters, so they tend to be creative and innovative. Aries want what they want, and they want it right away. They start new projects with ease but may have trouble completing them. They struggle when their projects don't yield immediate results, and they work best when they receive instant gratification. Instead of tackling a long project with no rewards until the end, an Aries should set smaller milestones so they can feel encouraged by reaping smaller rewards along the way to the finish line of the full project. It is very important for this sign not to take on too much, only to burn out when they run out of energy.

Since Aries is the youngest fire sign, Aries individuals might have the most trouble controlling their inner fire. They have a short fuse and are quick to anger, but they recover and get over their problems just as fast.

Leo (Simha)

After Aries or Mesha, the next fire sign in Vedic astrology is Leo or Simha. As the middle children of the fire signs, Leos can control the fire element in themselves a bit better than Aries. Leos are courageous, generous, loyal, vain, and dominant.

They can be overbearing because they need to be in charge, and they are susceptible to flattery since they are so proud.

Leo individuals thrive on attention, which can be both positive and negative for their spiritual growth. While most others quite literally fear public speaking or performing in front of a critical crowd more than death, Leos embraces the limelight and they enjoy having all eyes on them.

Leos can teach the other signs not to care so much about the opinions of others and to be bold and fearless. Leos are dreamers with big goals for themselves, so they can inspire others to reach for the stars as well.

But too much pride can lead to stubbornness or approval-seeking behavior, both of which can be downfalls for Leos. They can also use their pride to bully others or make them feel inadequate if they aren't careful.

Sagittarius (Dhanus)

As the final fire sign in Vedic astrology, Sagittarius or Dhanus is the most mature and controlled of all the fire signs. Although Sagittarians may lack a balance of other elements on their birth charts, overall, they might come across to others as more balanced than their fellow fire signs, Aries and Leo. They are the wisest and most patient of the fire signs.

The fire in Sagittarians shines through their optimism, sunny personality, and generally happy disposition. Sagittarians are extremely resilient, and when they get knocked down, they get back up again quickly with a smile on their face.

They are quite restless and embrace change and new experiences. They are fair-minded and philosophical, and can be very enterprising. Sagittarians hate hypocrisy, and they can be a bit overconfident and blunt.

Although they are admired by many thanks to their positive attitudes and adventurous spirits, Sagittarians can be somewhat unlucky in love because of their reluctance to commit. Like all fire signs, they value their freedom and independence. In Sagittarius this manifests not only when it comes to committing to a partner, but also to staying in one place.

They don't like to stay in one location, job, or relationship for too long because their inner fire makes them naturally restless. They yearn for adventure and need to explore new places and people frequently to be fulfilled.

Earth (Prithvi)

The earth element rules three signs in Vedic astrology: Taurus (Vrishabha), Virgo (Kanya), and Capricorn (Makara). Mercury is the primary ruler of the fire signs and is the sole ruler of Virgo. Venus and Saturn are also earth planets but to a lesser extent, and are the guiding heavenly bodies of Taurus and Capricorn, respectively.

Characteristics

The earth element represents stability, loyalty, and diligence. Earth is a grounding force that provides peace, balance, and the ability to work hard to achieve one's dreams. It is also the source of all plant life, and thus a very nourishing and nurturing element. Earth signs are gentle yet powerful, and graceful yet strong. Earth encourages growth in others and is a necessary building block towards any goal or aspiration.

Individuals born under the earth signs Taurus, Virgo, and Capricorn tend to be serious, ambitious, reliable, sturdy, resilient, and stoic. They are the wallflowers that you might not notice when they are present, but they are so important and crucial to making things work that you will surely notice when they are gone. They are excellent team members and work hard to perfect any task they are assigned. When you want a job done thoroughly and correctly, you should ask an earth sign to take care of it.

Since the earth is the force of all life and generation, earth sign individuals are tough and irrepressible. They are self-motivated and career-driven, and nothing can stop them from achieving their goals. When forces work against them, they only retreat for a period of new growth. Then they return and bloom again, stronger and more beautiful than before.

Imbalances

In the body, the earth element relates to food and what we use to nourish our physical selves. Mentally, earth gives us strength, logic, and the desire to succeed. An imbalance of earth in the mind can lead to a lack of emotional development or expression.

An imbalance of earth can affect a person's personality and disposition as well as the body. Too much earth causes slowness, physical violence, doggedness, greed, materialism, dullness, and overindulgence. It can also cause burnout from working too hard, or it can make a person neglect their relationships by focusing solely on career and finances.

A lack of earth makes people overly excitable, nervous, and unstable. They are lazy and lack ambition, and they have a hard time finishing any project they start or keeping their commitments. They may have metabolic issues and wild eyes.

The Signs

Taurus (Vrishaba)

While they are all ruled by the earth element, earth manifests differently in each of the three earth signs. The earth characteristics shine through each sign in many positive and negative ways.

As the zodiac sign ruled by Venus, Taurus is a very loving sign that expresses the earth element in romantic and interpersonal relationships. The earth in Taurus manifests as loyalty, patience, and sensuality in love. Venus also makes Taurus a lover of beauty, and combined with the earth element, a Taurus individual is likely skilled at gardening and cultivating flowers and plants.

The earth element makes these individuals extraordinarily hard workers. They are motivated by their desire for beautiful and luxurious material goods, such as expensive homes and designer clothes. Since Taurus people are very stubborn and diligent, nothing will stop them once they set their minds to something. Unlike their predecessor in the zodiac, Aries, a Taurus individual has the patience to see projects through to completion. This earth sign understands that the day you plant the seed is not the day you harvest the fruit. They don't rely on instant gratification, but instead set their sights on long-term goals. They do their best work when the results are tangible, such as money in their bank accounts or extravagant gifts. Praise is not as meaningful to them as a physical reward. They are good at conserving their energy and distributing it evenly from start to finish of a task, but they may not have any left to take care of themselves.

Since Taurus is the youngest earth sign, Taurus individuals might have the most trouble controlling and balancing their inner earth. They can dig their heels into the ground when they feel strongly about an issue, and they can hold grudges for eternity.

Virgo (Kanya)

After Taurus, the next earth sign in Vedic astrology is Virgo or Kanya. As the middle children of the earth signs or the second oldest, Virgos are more in control of the earth element in themselves than Taurus. In fact, Virgos exercise control in everything they do, which is typical of the earth element.

Virgo is symbolized by a flower or the virgin, often with a flower in her hair. This very symbol reveals the earthy, nurturing nature of this zodiac sign. Represented by the virgin, Virgo embodies the more feminine, nurturing side of earth signs.

They can be perfectionists because they are so meticulous and detail-oriented, and they might get stuck on the small details instead of looking at the bigger picture.

Virgo individuals tend to be introverted, introspective, and modest, which can be both positive and negative for their spiritual growth. They keep their feelings to themselves, unwilling to burden others with their troubles. But an analytical Virgo has a wealth of information and useful opinions that others could benefit from hearing, if the Virgo was willing to open up.

Virgos are very clever and logical, and you could never accuse one of being lazy. They work hard and do lots of research before making any decisions. They are cautious rather than impulsive, and timid instead of thrill-seeking.

But sometimes a Virgo can be a bit too proud, especially if their birth date is close to being its proud predecessor in the order of the zodiac, the fire sign Leo. Proud Virgos can't admit their flaws and might drive themselves (and others) crazy trying to make everything perfect. Virgos need to learn that nothing is perfect, and that the greatest beauty lies in imperfections.

Capricorn (Makara)

As the final or oldest earth sign in Vedic astrology, Capricorn or Makara is the most mature and controlled of the trio. They are the wisest and most patient of the earth signs, and one of the sagest signs of the entire zodiac. If Virgo represents feminine earth energy, then Capricorn is the masculine side of earth energy. Where Virgo is nurturing and caring, Capricorn is strict and punishing.

The earth in Capricorns shines through their ambition, aloofness, and drive to succeed. In fact, success and financial wealth can be an addiction to Capricorns.

They worry about what others think of them and care a great deal about their reputations. Their drive to succeed is partially motivated by fear. They fear failure as well as the negative perception and judgments it could bring them.

They are extremely cautious, but they are willing to take big risks if the rewards are great enough. Because they are so cold and calculating, Capricorns tend to come off as stoic and unfeeling.

But deep down, Capricorns are secretly quite sensitive. Their guardedness is again caused by fear. They fear embarrassing themselves or getting their hearts broken, so they build an emotional wall so high and strong that few attempt to penetrate them. Capricorns tend to value material things and their careers more than anything else because it's something they can see and control.

Capricorns think that they won't be fulfilled until they achieve their dreams, but true fulfillment for them lies in overcoming their many hidden fears and insecurities. They also must learn that relationships and emotions are more important than money, success, perfection, or being right.

Air (Vayu)

The air element rules three signs in Vedic astrology: Gemini (Mithuna), Libra (Tula), and Aquarius (Kumbha). Saturn is the primary ruler of the air signs and is one of the rulers of Aquarius, along with Uranus. Mercury and Venus are also airy planets but to a lesser extent, and are the guiding heavenly bodies of Gemini and Libra, respectively.

Characteristics

Each of the three air signs have distinctive characteristics, but they all share many traits as well. Air signs are generally social, outgoing, intellectual, and curious. They have a thirst for knowledge and a desire to understand the deeper meanings of things.

Air signs tend to be dreamy and easily swayed, as is the nature of this natural element. They can present or hear a sound logical argument in one direction, then give or believe the opposite argument if the reasoning is equally sound. They are fair-minded and value truth, justice, and equality.

Since air gives humans the ability to speak, air signs are highly communicative and talkative. They believe that every problem can be solved through communication, negotiation, and mutual understanding.

Air signs are friendly, charming, and adapt well to change. They are highly creative and philosophical, and are talented at coming up with new ideas and innovative ways of thinking.

Imbalances

Although there are many positive aspects to air signs, there are some negative ones that are manifested when the air element is out of balance.

When imbalanced, air signs can become so practical and rational that they forget about their emotions and intuition. They must learn to understand that some of the most important things, such as love, cannot be qualified or rationalized. They must also learn to embrace their feelings and express them productively instead of burying or ignoring them. Avoiding their emotions for too long can leave the air sign stuck in one place.

Since air signs are all about communication, imbalanced air signs might find themselves talking in circles and getting caught up in negotiations rather than taking real actions to achieve their goals. They can also make false promises and tell lies when imbalanced.

The Signs

Gemini (Mithuna)

Gemini, or Mithuna, is the first or youngest of the three air signs, meaning that it is the least mature and the air element is the least controlled.

Perhaps this lack of control is to blame for the deceptive nature of Gemini individuals. Symbolized by the twins, there are two sides to every Gemini. At best, this means they have hidden strengths, talents, and abilities unbeknownst even to themselves that can appear as needed in times of difficulty. At worst, their duality makes Geminis sneaky, underhanded, deceptive, unpredictable, and secretive.

Like Virgo, Gemini is guided by the planet Mercury. Mercury is the planet of intellect and communication, and combined with Gemini's airy nature, makes Geminis very smooth talkers. They can be charming, pleasant, and entertaining, or they can be witty, persuasive, and flattering.

The dual nature of a Gemini tells us that individuals born under this sign change their minds easily, and they can shift personalities as quickly as the weather changes. If they don't work on their personal development and growth, Geminis can become shallow and superficial. They may talk a lot about their plans, dreams, and talents, but without balancing forces, they will never take enough action to turn these dreams into a reality.

Libra (Tula)

It makes sense that Libra or Tula is the second or middle child of the air signs, situated comfortably between Gemini and Aquarius, because Libras strive for perfect balance and harmony in everything they do.

Libra is one of the few zodiac signs not represented by an animal, which may speak to the unemotional nature of this sign. Instead of an animal, human, or mythical creature, Libra is represented by the scales.

While all air signs value fairness and equality, being represented by the scales makes this trait even stronger in Libras. Many Libras find themselves in careers related to law, such as a judge, lawyer, or law enforcement.

Like the earth sign Taurus, Libra is guided by Venus. It makes sense that Libra shares its planet because Libra is a very generous and giving sign. The influence of Venus also makes Libras very loving and romantic. The combination of these traits means that, when out of balance, Libras tend to compromise and sacrifice themselves for the sake of others. This is especially true for Libras who are close to being Virgos, the earth sign just before Libra.

Libra individuals are often blessed with good looks, or at least a warm, open appearance and countenance that attracts others to them like magnets. Libras can connect and get along with almost anyone, and like their fellow air sign Gemini, they thrive in social settings.

Venus' influence not only makes Libras kind and loving but also gives them a keen eye for aesthetics. If they don't pursue a career in law, many Libras combine their innate communication skills with their aesthetic abilities by working in marketing or public relations.

When in balance, Libras are kind, caring, considerate, principled, and moral. They are natural peacemakers and work hard to resolve issues through communication and negotiation rather than force or violence. When out of balance, Libras are shallow, superficial, and materialistic. They struggle with making any decisions, no matter how great or small, important or inconsequential. They procrastinate a lot and are prone to anxiety and depression.

Aquarius (Kumbha)

The final air sign is Aquarius, or Kumbha, making it the oldest and most mature of the air signs. Aquarius is also the penultimate sign of the entire zodiac, making it one of the wisest and most spiritually experienced signs. Although one of Aquarius' ruling planets is Saturn, making it the strongest representation of the air element signs, Aquarius is perhaps the least like its fellow air signs Gemini and Libra.

This is largely because Aquarians are more likely to be introverted than their fellow air signs. The social nature portrayed by air signs manifests in a concern and care for society and all of humanity rather than a desire to attend parties or plan social events.

While Aquarians are very logical and practical like the other air signs, they are more in touch with their intuition. They possess old souls and a worldly wisdom that can only be gained over time. They care more about others and the greater good than themselves, and they are very open-minded and progressive thinkers.

They use their social skills to convince people, almost with a sense of urgency, to stop their destructive and reckless habits and start caring about the planet and the rest of society. They are very quirky and unique, and they aren't afraid to let their differences shine.

In balance, Aquarians are passionate, logical, resilient, inventive, and innovative. They are very generous, particularly when it comes to their loved ones or a worthy cause. When out of balance, they become careless, depressed, moody, stubborn, and contrary. They can put up emotional walls that prevent them from connecting with their loved ones, and they may suffer from anxiety and depression due to their profound care for the state of the world.

Water (Jal)

The water element rules three signs in Vedic astrology: Cancer (Karkata), Scorpio (Vrishik), and Pisces (Meena). The Moon, Pluto, and Neptune are the celestial bodies associated with the water signs, ruling Cancer, Scorpio, and Pisces, respectively.

Characteristics

All of the water signs have certain traits in common, but they each have distinctive personality traits, as well. Water signs are emotional, pensive, moody, serious, and complex. They experience their emotions profoundly and are highly creative and intuitive. They may come off as sneaky or aloof, but really they are just private and mysterious. Water signs are the most likely to possess psychic abilities due to their keen sense of intuition and their ability to connect with their spirituality.

Water signs can teach the rest of the zodiac to be more in touch with their feelings and honor their emotions. They value emotional expression in any form, especially through music, poetry, dance, and art.

Imbalances

Like any of the elements, an imbalance of water can lead to many problems. Too much water in the birth chart can make someone emotionally dependent, needy, and clingy. It can also make them overly sensitive, extremely emotional, and moody.

Too much water can lead to addiction, overindulgence, escapism, paranoia, and emotional outbursts. It creates an unhealthy focus on feelings over logic and reason. Too little water or an imbalanced water sign can cause emotional detachment, an inability to connect with others, a lack of compassion, and insensitivity.

The Signs

Cancer (Karkata)

Cancer is the first water sign and perhaps represents the earth element in its crudest, rawest form. As the youngest and least mature of the three water signs, Cancers tend to struggle with emotional regulation and self-control. Cancer individuals are likely to throw tantrums, burst into tears, or have angry outbursts because their souls haven't yet learned how to handle the intense way they experience their emotions.

Guided by the Moon, Cancer represents feminine, nurturing energy. Cancer is the sign of the Mother, so Cancers are caring, graceful, and extremely loving.

Cancers are perhaps the most likely of the three zodiac signs to struggle with romantic relationships because they form such intense, close emotional bonds so quickly. If their partner isn't as emotionally developed or attached, it can deeply hurt a Cancer.

As a result of heartbreak, they may swing wildly to the other side of the emotional spectrum, attempting to close themselves off from true love. Once they accept that their vulnerability is their greatest strength, and that it inherently comes with great risks, they can become their best selves.

Cancers would be lucky to find a forever love early on in life, but this may not allow for Cancers to grow into the best individuals they can be. It is through hardships, heartbreaks, and sacrifices that they can evolve into their highest forms.
This doesn't mean that the life of a Cancer is all doom and gloom. Although they are the Mothers of the zodiac, in many ways, Cancers are childlike. They embrace the world and all it has to offer wholeheartedly, yet at the same time, they put a great deal of effort into cultivating their homes and their families. They provide comfort and peace to their loved ones, and while they are fiercely protective, they draw out the protective nature in others, as well.

Scorpio (Vrishtik)

Scorpio or Vrishtik is the second water sign of the zodiac, making it the middle child of the water signs. Scorpio is perhaps the most different from its fellow water signs, largely due to its guiding planets. Unlike most signs, Scorpio has not just one but two ruling heavenly bodies, making this zodiac sign quite complex.

Scorpio is ruled by both Pluto, the planet of death, life, transformation, and power, and Mars, the planet of war, conflict, passion, competition, and aggression. These planetary influences make Scorpio a very unique, powerful, and intense sign.

The combined influences of Pluto and Mars makes Scorpios controlling. They are very deliberate and careful in nearly everything they do, except for the rare, planned moments when they give themselves permission to let loose.

Scorpios need to learn to relinquish control and accept what the universe brings them. They especially need to give up control in their personal relationships. Like the fellow water sign Cancer, love is very important to Scorpios, but challenges arise when they try to dominate their partners too much.

Pisces (Meena)

Pisces is the final and oldest of the three water signs, and it is also the very last sign of the zodiac. It has a balance of both feminine and masculine energies but is still largely feminine. If its predecessor, Aquarius, has the soul of a wise old man, then Pisces has the soul of a genderless being with one foot in the earthly realm and the other already in the next, spiritual world.

If water element zodiac signs are the most likely to be psychic, then Pisces is the most likely of them all to possess supernatural gifts. Pisces individuals are not only very in touch with their emotions but they are also closely connected with the spiritual realm.

They may have big goals and ambitions, but their concerns aren't so much materialistic as they are spiritual.

Pisces people yearn to take the lessons from the ages and apply them to this world so that they can have a better existence in the next life.

Pisces individuals experience their emotions very profoundly, but unlike fellow water signs Cancer and Scorpio, Pisces does not struggle as much with emotional regulation and self-control. As the most mature sign of the zodiac, a Pisces has already mastered lessons in discipline and is completely unafraid of emotional expression and vulnerability.

Pisces is a very patient and generous teacher, but Pisces must be firm and protect themselves from trusting the wrong people. They can change their minds easily, so they must not allow themselves to be influenced by the wrong people with bad intentions. Pisces in balance is dedicated, kind, and helpful. Out of balance, Pisces people are erratic, lazy, and lack direction. They are also prone to depression and addiction.

Space (Akasa)

In Vedic astrology, the space element, also known as the ether, is different from the other four elements. It encompasses all of the elements, yet at the same time, it is completely separate.

The space element relates to awareness and consciousness. It is the layer beyond the four physical elements, and therefore does not correlate with any zodiac signs.

Space is related to freedom, thought processes, perception, and reaching our truest, highest versions of ourselves. Since it represents freedom from the body and even the mind, space is beyond our physical karma.

The space element allows us to acknowledge and experience the oneness of nature and the connectedness of the universe as a whole.

Chapter Four: The Planets (Navagrahas)

The planets, called the Navagrahas, are viewed as having significant influence over the signs in Vedic astrology. Each zodiac sign has one or two dominating planets, with some planets shared between two signs.

Although each individual person belongs to a zodiac sign with an oriental planet (the planet rising just before the sun in your chart), everyone is influenced by all of the planets in different ways. The position of the planets on the birth chart and which mansions they are in reveal your personality and how the planets will affect you throughout the course of your life. This is how the space element affects every birth chart.

The planets and the signs they rule:

Sun - Leo
Moon - Cancer
Mars - Aries and, to a lesser extent, Scorpio
Mercury - Gemini and Virgo
Jupiter - Sagittarius and, to a lesser extent, Pisces
Venus - Taurus and Libra
Saturn - Capricorn and, to a lesser extent, Aquarius
Northern Lunar Node
Southern Lunar Node

All of the planets have both positive and negative aspects to their energies. The effects of the planets are largely determined by their placement on your birth chart and their relationships to one another on the chart.

Some of the planets are considered "beneficial" planets, meaning they are generally viewed as lucky and prosperous, regardless of the zodiac signs. The beneficial planets are Mercury, Jupiter, and Venus.

There are also "detrimental" planets, or planets with a mostly negative influence. These planets are the Sun, Mars, Saturn, and the Northern and Southern Lunar Nodes.

Although the Lunar Nodes are viewed as detrimental, the Moon is typically considered neutral, having no particularly positive or negative effect. Depending on the value assigned to the Moon, it can have either a beneficial or detrimental effect.

Some Vedic astrologers believe that there are no detrimental or beneficial planets because they all work in harmony together. One set of planets could not be beneficial if the others weren't detrimental, so all forces are equally necessary. Those that are considered "detrimental" perhaps just need to be balanced by the "beneficial" planets.

Mars, Jupiter, Mercury, Venus, and Saturn all have retrograde periods, which is when they appear to move backward in the sky. The effects of these planets while in retrograde are very different from their usual effects. The Sun and Moon do have retrogrades.

The Dashas

Dashas, or planetary periods, are based on the time of birth and affect all aspects of life from the moment of birth until death. Maha-Dashas are longer periods of time that are broken down into smaller sub-periods. This helps keep you balanced, so even if you are in a Maha-Dasha ruled by a detrimental or unfriendly planet, you can still experience shorter periods that are ruled by beneficial or friendly planets. Vedic astrology is all about accepting the natural ebb and flow, so there will always be periods of grace and reprieve even in long stretches of tough times.

The Gocharas

The movements of the planets have a special effect known as Gocharas, and like the Dashas, they have a lifelong influence. For example, the effects of the waning and waxing of the moon are considered Gocharas. As the moon appears fuller in the night sky, it has the effect of making us feel inspired, creative, restless, and active. When the moon wanes or appears to decrease in size, it's a time of rest, reflection, and restoration.

Drishti

Drishti is a term that you will see used in other ways, such as in yoga as a point of focus. The Sanskrit word literally translates to "sight," and in Vedic astrology, it refers to the effect of the planets affecting the houses they see. Picture a planet surveying the houses from the heavens, and those houses being affected just by being in that planet's "sight."

Yoga

When you read the word yoga, the first thing that comes to mind is probably breathing exercises or a series of physical movements. But in Vedic astrology, "yoga" refers to the effect of the planets in relation to each other, according to their placements.

The Sun (Surya)

In Vedic astrology, the sun is considered a planet rather than a star or other celestial body. The Sun is the king or ruler, and represents masculine energy, paternity, and royalty. The temperament of the Sun is hot, fiery, angry, and fierce. The colors associated with the Sun are red, yellow, and orange. The Sun's associated metal is gold, and its gem is the ruby. The Sun rules over Sunday.

The Sun stays in each sign for a month and takes a year to complete a full cycle around the entire zodiac, and its modality or motion is fixed. The Sun's movement rules the zodiac because it dictates when each sign ends and begins. The movement of the Sun also dictates the changing of seasons.

The Moon (Chandra)

Like the Sun, the Moon is considered a royal, regal planet and complementary to the Sun. If the Sun is the king planet, then the Moon is the queen in Vedic astrology. The Moon's qualities and effects are the perfect foil to the Sun. Where the Sun is masculine, the Moon is feminine. While the Sun is hot and angry, the Moon is cool and calm.

The Moon also represents the Mother, and relates to emotions, intuition, sensitivity, compassion, the home, water, comfort, and hospitality. The Moon is associated with the color white, silver metal, and the pearl gemstone. The Moon rules Monday.

The Moon is the fastest moving of the nine planets in Vedic astrology, spending about two to three days to travel through each sign. When the Sun and the Moon are in the same place, it is called Amavasya or New Moon Day. The lunar days, called Tithi, change with every 12-degree difference between the Sun and Moon. When the Sun and the Moon are 180 degrees apart or in opposite signs, this is called Poornima or the Full Moon Day.

Mars (Mangala, Kuja)

Mars, also known as Mangala or Kuja, is the commander or general of astrology. Picture the Sun king and the Moon queen with Mars serving as their brother and the head of the army. Mars represents strength, energy, bravery, courage, younger siblings, armed forces, police, authority figures, and high positions. The metal associated with Mars is copper, the gemstone is coral, and the color for Mars is red. Mars spends about 45 days in each zodiac sign. Mars rules over Tuesday.

Mercury (Budha)

If the Sun and Moon are the king and queen of astrology, Mercury or Budha is the prince or uncle. Mercury symbolizes communication, intellect, travel, marketing, commerce, technology, journalism, books, and even astrology itself. The metal associated with mercury is bronze, the gemstone is the emerald, and the lucky color is green. Mercury spends about one month or 30 days in each zodiac sign, and it is always 27-degrees away from the Sun. Mercury is the ruler of Wednesday.

Jupiter (Guru, Brihaspati)

Jupiter, also called Guru or Brihaspati, is known as the guru of the Gods, or "Devaguru." The planet Jupiter symbolizes learning, knowledge, priesthood, churches, instructors, specialists, experts, researchers, scientists, students, and children. The color for Jupiter is yellow, its metal is gold (shared with the Sun), and the gemstone is the yellow sapphire. Jupiter spends approximately one year in each sign. Jupiter rules over Thursday.

Venus (Shukra)

Venus, or Shukra, is complementary to Jupiter and is the guru of the demons, known as "Daityaguru." Venus stands for love, marriage, beauty, spouses, sexuality, the arts, dancing, music, acting, gemstones, crystals, alcohol, and fashion. The metal associated with Venus is silver (shared with the Moon), the gemstone is the diamond, and the color is white. Venus spends about one month in each sign, traveling through each of the 12 signs once in a one-year period. Venus is always 48-degrees from the Sun. Venus rules over Friday.

Saturn (Shani)

Saturn, or Shani, is the servant in astrology. Saturn represents workers, laborers, hardship, and sorrow. The placement of Saturn on the birth chart can dictate whether an individual is blessed with great power, fame, and fortune, or if that person is doomed to failure, devastation, and suffering. The metal for Saturn is iron, the power color is blue, and its gemstone is the blue sapphire. While the Sun is the fastest moving of the planets in Vedic astrology, Saturn is the slowest. Saturn takes about two to three years to travel through each zodiac sign, taking about 30 years to traverse through all 12 signs. The "Saturn Return," or each 30-year period in a person's life, when Saturn returns to the position it was in when you were born, is highly significant. Thus, the ages around 30, 60, 90, and 120 and the experiences you have at those ages are related to Saturn. Saturn is the ruler of Saturday.

North Lunar Node (Rahu)

While the Moon is its own planet, in Vedic astrology, we must also consider the Northern and Southern lunar Nodes. The North Node, also known as Rahu or the Dragon's Head, represents foreign lands, strangers, foreigners, international travel, smoke, grandparents, elderly people, rebels, the underworld, and the seedy, bad underbelly of society. The color of the North Node is black and the gemstone is hessonite. Rahu spends about one to one and half years in each zodiac sign, completing a full transit through all 12 signs every 18 years. Neither of the Lunar Nodes rules a day of the week.

The North Node, or ascending node, is where the Moon crosses the ecliptic going toward the northern hemisphere, and the South Node, or descending node, is where the Moon crosses the ecliptic going south. The North Node and the South Node are always directly opposite one another in the sky.

South Lunar Node (Ketu)

The Southern Lunar Node, also known as Ketu or the Dragon's Tail, stands for spirituality and superstitions. The color of the South Node is brown, and the gemstone is chrysoberyl. Ketu is always opposite of Rahu, exactly 180-degrees apart. Like Rahu, Ketu takes about one to one and half years to travel through the signs, moving through all 12 signs every 18 years. Like Rahu, Ketu does not rule a day of the week.

Chapter Five: The Lunar Mansions (Nakshatras)

In Vedic astrology, there are not only twelve "houses," as there are in Western astrology, but there are also twenty-seven lunar "mansions," which aren't to be confused with the houses.

This is one of the most significant distinctions between Western astrology and Vedic astrology because it has to do with the sidereal system, which is used in Vedic but not Western astrology, and explains how the same zodiac signs correspond to different dates in the two systems.

In Vedic astrology, the Moon spends one day of each month in each of the 27 lunar mansions. Vedic astrology assigns much greater importance to the Moon, distinguishing it from Western astrology, which focuses on the Sun. Knowing which lunar mansion the Moon was visiting during your time of birth can reveal a great deal about your personality, motivations, and destiny.

Here are the 27 lunar mansions, their Vedic names, and their significance:

1. Ashvini

Ashvini or Aswini is also known as the Horse Goddess and is affiliated with the zodiac sign Aries. If you were born while the Moon was in this lunar mansion, you likely have a zest for life, a rebellious streak, and difficulty staying still. You get bored easily so you need constant mental and physical stimulation. You're not one to follow the crowd and go along with what everyone else is doing, but rather, you come up with new ideas and challenge old ways of thinking. You crave adventure, yearn for excitement, and actively seek adrenaline rushes. You are bold and willing to take risks in every aspect of your life, and sometimes your recklessness and impulsivity can get you into trouble.

Speed and efficiency are far more important to you than accuracy and perfection, but you must remember that there is a time and place for these preferences and they won't always work in your favor. You are a pioneer and a natural leader, and you prefer being in an authority position over following rules and obeying authority. You may struggle with taking on or accepting responsibility because you are such a free spirit. You are youthful, playful, and humorous, but you can also be vain and arrogant. You are also prone to angry outbursts and temper tantrums when you don't get your way, and you can be a bit overbearing and bossy. You are a natural healer and have special gifts relating to herbs and medicine.

2. Bharni

Bharni or Bharani, also known as the River of Souls, is also affiliated with the zodiac sign Aries. If you were born while the Moon was in this lunar mansion, you may have a mercurial and turbulent personality. You are likely creative, artistic, and sensual, with a strong passionate side and even stronger convictions. While you may create or find yourself in difficult situations, you are determined, resilient, and skilled at solving problems, so you can overcome any obstacles that stand in your path.

You are compassionate and empathetic, so you feel and care deeply for others, especially your loved ones. Willpower and self-control are your greatest tools, and you must hone these skills in order to overcome the challenges that come your way in life. Bharni is also known as the soul traveler, so you likely have a mystical, ethereal, shamanic side.

3. Krittika

Krittika or Krittica is known as the Star of Fire, and is associated with the zodiac signs Aries and Taurus. Being born while the Moon transits this lunar mansion means that you are extremely honest, sometimes to a fault. You may hurt people with your criticisms and unkind words if you aren't careful.

You are hard-working, ambitious, and self-motivated, and you make a strong leader as long as your impulsivity and recklessness don't get the best of you. You have a profound presence and are quite serious, but you can also be witty, imaginative, and playful. You have a close relationship with food and probably enjoy cooking. You must watch your weight as you likely have a strong appetite, so you should focus on learning how to cook healthy foods. You are also highly compassionate and innately nurturing, so you tend to take care of the people around you.

4. Rohini

Rohini is also known as the Red Goddess, and is affiliated with the zodiac sign Taurus. Being born while the Moon visits this lunar mansion makes you beautiful, attractive, magnetic, sensual, charming, and creative. You are romantic and drawn to superficial beauty, including beauty in nature, and you are a fan of the arts. You probably have a skill or strong passion related to singing, acting, dancing, drawing, painting, or playing a musical instrument. One of these artistic endeavors may be your career path, and you thrive when you have a productive form of creative expression to release your emotions.

You are very honest and careful with your words because you appreciate precise language, and you can be highly critical of yourself and others. You have strong views and convictions, but you also have a philosophical side that is open to new ideas and ways of thinking. You love luxury and comfort, but at the same time, you are earthy and unafraid to get your hands dirty. You are quite practical and logical, but you must take care not to quell your emotional side. You must also avoid focusing on superficial, worldly things and becoming too materialistic because it will lead you to a life of dissatisfaction.

5. Mrigashirsha

Mrigashirsha is also known as Orion, the Star of Searching, and is related to the zodiac signs Taurus and Gemini. If you were born when the Moon visits this lunar mansion, then you have a powerful, passionate, and restless personality. You seek truth and enjoy learning new things, so you are always researching and taking classes. You are a strong communicator with special skills related to writing, speaking, or story-telling. You are indecisive and can easily change your mind, so your views and opinions shift frequently. You may come off as moody or sneaky because you aren't firm in your convictions. You are gentle, kind, and sensual, but you are also prone to overindulgence and greed. You enjoy travel and embrace change, but you avoid confrontation and have a hard time settling down.

6. Ardra

Ardra or Aarudhra is also known as the Tear Drop and is connected to the zodiac sign Gemini. Being born when the Moon visits this lunar mansion gives you a stormy, emotional, turbulent personality. You feel your emotions profoundly, are a deep thinker, and possess strong communication skills. You have the ability to be highly successful but you must develop patience and work hard in order to succeed. You can be a bit impulsive, belligerent, and destructive at times, especially when you are feeling out of control and out of balance. Your innate thirst for knowledge and intellectual curiosity make you an excellent student, teacher, writer, or speaker.

7. Punarvasu

Punarvasu or Punavasu, also known as the Light Bringer, correlates with the zodiac signs Gemini and Cancer. If Ardra, the previous lunar mansion, is stormy and turbulent, then this lunar mansion is the calm that comes after the storm. Being born while the Moon transits this lunar mansion makes you friendly, easy-going, and adaptive. You make friends easily and generally go with the flow. You are philosophical and spiritual, with a deep appreciation for the arts, particularly poetry and painting. You are highly sensitive in that you experience emotions profoundly, are strongly affected by your surroundings, and are compassionate to the needs of others around you.

You value your home, friends, and family more than anything else in life, and you love to travel and have fun. You are a people-pleaser, and sometimes your need to appease everyone can get you into trouble. You may exhaust yourself bending over backward for everyone else or be accused of being disloyal because you can see multiple points of view. You aren't materialistic, but you cherish your house and possessions with sentimental attachments.

8. Pushya

Pushya, also known as Nourishment, is connected to the zodiac sign Cancer. If you were born when the Moon transits this lunar mansion, you are supportive, maternal, caring, and helpful. You enjoy nurturing and cultivating people, plants, and animals, and you are the person friends and family members turn to for comfort and protection. You are mature and wise beyond your years, and probably often are told that you're an "old soul."

You have strong moral values and integrity, so it's important to you to always do the right thing, even when no one else is watching. You are sensitive but exert control over your emotional reactions, so you are good at expressing how you feel in productive ways. You must watch out for becoming too stubborn, rigid, and traditional in your views. You thrive when you work hard and can use your creativity to further humanitarian goals and help others.

9. Aslesha

Aslesha, also known as the Coiled Serpent, is affiliated with the zodiac sign Cancer. Being born while the Moon visits this serpentine lunar mansion makes you wise and shrewd. Your powers derive from looking into the darkest corners of the soul. You embrace darkness in times when others fear it or push it away because you are wise enough to know that there cannot be light without darkness, a lesson that many others fail to understand.

You are thoughtful, philosophical, analytical, and serious, and you are highly independent and a bit reclusive. You are likely an introvert and get your energy from being alone, and you probably find crowds and being around other people for too long draining. You are sensual and intuitive, and you may even possess psychic powers. Be careful not to let the darkness overtake you, but to continue observing and accepting it from a peaceful distance.

10. Magha

Magha, also known as the Forefathers, correlates with the zodiac sign Leo. If you were born when the Moon visits this lunar mansion, you likely have a strong, regal presence and are very proud. When you enter a room, others immediately notice you because you possess the majestic dignity of royalty. You may be conservative and traditional in your views and following the path of your ancestors is important to you.

You have a big personality and are likely generous, compassionate, and sensual. You may be a bit restless and turbulent, and you must be careful not to get too hungry for wealth, power, or status. These things ultimately won't fulfill you and will only make you a worse person. If you focus on striving for contentment rather than worldly success, you have the potential for greatness.

11. Purva Phalguni

Purva Phalguni, also known as the World Tree Goddess, is associated with the zodiac sign Leo. Being born while the Moon visits this lunar mansion makes love, romance, and marriage of the utmost importance to you. You are at your best when in a happy relationship and you dislike being single or alone. You are passionate, sensual, affectionate, loving, and have an infectious zest for life. You are likely quite lucky and make friends easily thanks to your outgoing and diplomatic personality. You can be a bit narcissistic, impulsive, and overindulgent, so take care to avoid cultivating these qualities.

12. Uttara Phalguni

Uttara Phalguni, also known as the Marriage Goddess, correlates with the zodiac signs Leo and Virgo. Being born while the Moon visits this lunar mansion makes marriage, love, and romance important to you (as with the previous lunar mansion, Purva Phalguni), but there is a particular emphasis on sexuality.

You are attractive and possess a magnetic personality, and you are magnanimous and compassionate. You have a big heart and care a great deal about social justice and equality, so you will likely enter a profession that allows you to advocate for others in need. You hate being alone, so you must take care not to develop codependency in your relationships. You must also be selective when choosing partners, and try not to stay in relationships that inhibit your personal growth. You have a strong interest in the metaphysical or spiritual realm, and you are generally very lucky and tend to succeed in your endeavors.

13. Hasta

Hasta, also known as Skilled Activities, is related to the zodiac sign Virgo. If you were born while the Moon transits this lunar mansion, you have quite a complex personality. You are highly intelligent, creative, and hard-working, and thanks to your superior mental abilities, you are capable of mastering any skill you choose to pursue.

However, you are quite fickle and change your mind frequently, so you may flit from project to project without taking enough time to finish or conquer any of them completely. You must force yourself to choose your paths carefully and see them through to the end, lest you end up achieving nothing at the end of the day due to your vacillation. You have a kind and sympathetic side that you must nurture, and you should also put your innate creative abilities to use instead of ignoring them to focus solely on practical pursuits.

14. Chitra

Chitra, or the Jewel, corresponds with the zodiac signs Virgo and Libra. If you were born when the Moon visits this lunar mansion, you seek to impress and please others (or shine like a jewel). You possess natural poise, elegance, charisma, and leadership abilities. You want to stand out, but only in positive ways. You are quite competitive and yearn to be the best at everything you do. You are an analytical, logical thinker with a strong intellectual curiosity. You make an excellent student, and your ability to pick up new skills and absorb information can make you impatient with others who do not possess these gifts. While it's important for you to stand in your power and never dull your shine for anyone else, it is equally important for you to be gracious and avoid becoming arrogant and conceited.

15. Swati

Swati, also known as the Wind God, is associated with the zodiac sign Libra. If you were born while the Moon visits this lunar mansion, you are independent, restless, flexible, and adaptable. You have a light-hearted, bright personality that attracts others to you like a magnet. You love learning new skills and information, and you have a strong appreciation for the arts. You have some natural business skills and could be a great entrepreneur. You are generous and big-hearted, and you have a lot of integrity.

Your restlessness makes you a bit scatter-brained and easily distracted, so you must take care to focus on one thing at a time. You probably enjoy travel, as it gives you the opportunity to learn about new cultures and satisfy your restless spirit. You are physically fragile, so you must take special care of your health and give yourself plenty of time to rest and recharge.

16. Vishakha

Vishakha, also known as the Moon of Power, is affiliated with the zodiac signs Libra and Scorpio. Being born while the Moon visits this lunar mansion gives you a powerful presence and a strong personality. You are ambitious, competitive, brave, and fearless, and you have an innate drive to achieve ambitious goals.

While the previous lunar mansion, Swati, suffers from a lack of focus, you have such a one-track mind that you risk neglecting all other aspects of life while you focus so hard on one thing. You are prone to obsession, and you must schedule time for rest and relaxation so that you don't run out of energy. It's important for you to strive for balance in your life because you tend to take everything, both positives and negatives, to extremes. You are gifted with high intellect and the ability to research and absorb new information with ease. You must work on cultivating patience, and you should focus your intense energy and efforts on the greater good rather than selfish endeavors.

17. Anuradha

Anuradha, also known as the Moon of Friendship, correlates with the zodiac sign Scorpio. If you were born while the Moon visits this lunar mansion, you are likely cooperative and friendly, and you possess a special talent for dealing with people and making them like you. You make friends easily and can maintain lasting, close bonds.

You also have the potential to have wonderful romantic relationships that strengthen and fulfill you. You are passionate and gentle, yet bold and resilient. You're drawn to math, data, and statistics, and may have a career related to these fields. You are probably very clean and organized, and you enjoy travelling. You will experience the most success when you travel or settle away from your place of birth. You are extremely sensitive and vulnerable, so you can be volatile and temperamental at times. You are prone to fits of frustration and angry outbursts, and you will have to work on learning to control your emotional reactions. Remember that your sensitivity and vulnerability are strengths; it is only your reactions to these gifts that you must work on.

18. Jyeshtha

Jyeshtha, also known as the Wisdom Crone, is associated with the zodiac sign Scorpio. If you were born while the Moon transits this lunar mansion, you are highly self-disciplined and possess more self-control than most. This skill comes in handy when working to achieve your goals, but it can also make you self-punishing and self-depriving. You have a strong personality and are likely very controlling. You are crafty, deliberate, talented, analytical, and smart. You have a magical, ethereal side to your personality that you must take care to nourish and not overlook. You may be vain and easy to anger, and sometimes you retreat into yourself when your pride is wounded or you are suffering from low self-esteem. You are attracted to dark places where you can shine your light the brightest, and when in balance, you can be an excellent provider for others and a source of deep wisdom and strength.

19. Moola

Moola or Mula, also known as the Root of All Things, is connected to the zodiac sign Sagittarius. Being born while the Moon visits this lunar mansion makes you philosophical and inquisitive, and you yearn to find deeper meanings and get to the bottom of things. You are a careful and persistent researcher, and you would likely thrive in professional fields related to science and medicine.

You are also bold, charismatic, and persuasive, so you would do well in a public speaking position. You are passionate and need to feel strongly about your work to do a good job. You have a strong sense of intuition and you must follow your arrow where it points because your gut instincts will not lead you astray. At times you may feel stuck or trapped, and you must turn to philosophy and spirituality to escape this feeling instead of looking to worldly pleasures and material things for comfort.

20. Purvashada

Purvashada or Purva Ashadha, also known as the Moon of Early Victory, is associated with the zodiac sign Sagittarius. Being born while the Moon travels through this lunar mansion means that you will likely experience great success early in life. You are brave, strong, fearless, and charismatic, and you have the power of persuasion. You are great at debating and arguing, so you would make an excellent professional lawyer. Despite your power over others, you have a great deal of compassion and empathy. You are highly spiritual and philosophical, and you will develop great wisdom and resilience by going through struggles, particularly in adulthood. You must not allow your early success in life to make you lazy, arrogant, overindulgent, or materialistic.

21. Uttarashada

Uttarashada or Uttara Ashadha, also known as the Moon of Later Victory, is affiliated with both the Sagittarius and Capricorn zodiac signs. If you were born when the Moon visits this lunar mansion, you are idealistic and a humanitarian. You are honest and have strong moral values, and you care deeply about social justice.

You are ambitious, responsible, and refined, and you have lofty goals. Most of your success will come later in life once you have learned to balance your intense passion and restlessness with your bouts of carelessness and laziness. Making a name for yourself, being remembered after death, and creating a legacy are important to you, and you may find it impossible to achieve all of your ambitious goals. You have strong communication skills, and you are a great friend.

22. Shravana

Shravana, also known as the Moon of Listening, is connected to the zodiac sign Capricorn. Being born while the Moon visits this lunar mansion makes you wise, intelligent, and truth-seeking. You are an excellent student and would make a wonderful teacher, as well. You value knowledge that comes from oral traditions, story-telling, and experiences rather than new theories or abstract concepts. You are an avid reader and love books, so you might find yourself working in a bookstore or a library. You have an insatiable thirst for knowledge and you probably possess writing skills, as well. You are likely a sensitive, introverted person. You may have struggles and setbacks early in life, but will achieve success and have more positive experiences in adulthood.

23. Dhanishta

Dhanishta, also known as the Drummer, correlates with both the Capricorn and Aquarius zodiac signs. Being born while the Moon transits this lunar mansion makes you an optimistic, adventurous, and powerful person with a strong personality. You will likely have the most success away from your place of birth, and you like being in control. You must not allow your hunger for power make you selfish, greedy, materialistic, or arrogant. You must work on cultivating patience so that your innate generosity can shine through. You will thrive when you put your energy and enthusiasm towards helping the greater good rather than pursuing purely selfish ambitions.

24. Shatabhishak

Shatabhishak or Shatabhisha, also known as the Divine Healer, is associated with the zodiac sign Aquarius. If you were born while the Moon visits this lunar mansion, you are likely independent and introverted. You have a mystical, ethereal quality and a strong interest in all things spiritual and metaphysical. You are also intrigued by philosophy and psychology.

You enjoy solitude and can be a bit reclusive, needing plenty of time to yourself to explore your interests and recharge your energy. You get very absorbed in your work, and since you are highly intelligent with reading and writing skills, you are likely to be found with your nose in a book and your head in the clouds. You experience a great deal of trauma and extremes in life that allow you to heal and blossom into something greater, like a lotus rising from the mud or a phoenix from the ashes. You can turn a crisis or traumatic experience into a self-actualizing moment, and overcoming a serious health issue gives you healing powers.

25. Purva Bhadra

Purva Bhadra or Purva Bhadrapada, also known as the Fire Dragon, connects with the zodiac signs Aquarius and Pisces. Being born while the moon visits this lunar mansion makes you a unique, eccentric, quirky, and mystical individual. You care a great deal about social justice and commit yourself to social reform. You are a powerful and talented speaker, so you will likely use this gift to work towards your goals. You see both the good and bad in human nature, which makes you hopeful yet skeptical. You don't trust easily and you can be a bit critical and terse at times. Instead of focusing on the injustices of the world, you will thrive when you focus on working towards the greater good and uplifting those around you. You are a visionary and possess the power to transform yourself and others.

26. Uttara Bhadra

Uttara Bhadra or Uttara Bhadrapada, also known as the Dragon of the Deep, correlates with the zodiac sign Pisces. Being born when the Moon visits this lunar mansion makes you a skillful writer and speaker. You can be intense and passionate, but you possess the self-discipline and restraint to control your inner fire. You are a progressive thinker with a great deal of insight and clarity. You have an old soul and wisdom beyond your years. You are quite lucky, particularly in financial aspects, and you must be careful not to become too dependent on your good fortune. You can be very private and secretive, so you need lots of time to yourself and a quiet place to meditate and relax. You are intuitive and magical, and you must use these powers for the greater good instead of evil or selfish purposes.

27. Revati

Revati, also known as the Moon of Splendor, is the final lunar mansion and is affiliated with the zodiac sign Pisces. If you were born during the time when the Moon visits this lunar mansion, you are a king, nurturing, and caring person who feels a deep sense of responsibility for others. You are a compassionate humanitarian, and you believe you exist to serve others and the greater good. You probably do a lot of volunteer work and contribute money to several charities, and you likely enjoy being around animals, plants, and children.

You are blessed with financial fortune, but you don't care very much about material things. You are sensitive, vulnerable, and genuine, and you are also probably very creative and artistic. You may suffer some serious struggles early in life that teach you that the world can be a cruel place. You must not allow your negative, traumatic experiences to put out your inner light, for you are highly spiritual and a gift to the world. You must take care of yourself and not give so much to others that you have no time, energy, or resources left to nourish yourself with at the end of the day.

Chapter Six: The Houses (Bhavas)

In Western astrology, there are 12 "houses," one for each sign of the zodiac. The same is true for Vedic astrology; there are 12 houses, or Bhavas. But in Vedic astrology, there are also 27 lunar "mansions," and it is very important not to confuse the mansions with the houses, as they have very different and distinctive meanings.

The houses in Vedic astrology create the foundation of life. They divide and define the areas of one's life, and can be determined based on the birth chart. Together, the 12 houses form a 360-degree angle on the birth chart, with each house ruling one of 12 equal sections. It is important to distinguish the houses from the zodiac wheel, as each house is connected to a different zodiac sign based on an individual's birth chart, and each house represents a specific aspect of life.

Here are the 12 Bhavas and their associated meanings, characteristics, zodiac signs, body parts, and planets:

First house

The first house represents the self, self-image, and appearance. The first house rules the body, which dictates the way you look, your physique, physical strength, health, and fortitude. The first house relates to the ego and the sense of self.

This house affects your self-awareness, your knowledge of your own weaknesses and strengths, and your life choices. It is tied to your identity, preferences, attitude, perspective, and the way you wish others to perceive you.

The first house rules the head and face, including the skull, brain, hair, and facial features. According to Vedic astrology, if you have a weak first house, you may suffer from hair loss, acne, migraines, or frequent head injuries, but if your first house is strong, you will have full, luscious locks, high intelligence, or beautiful facial features.

The first house corresponds with Aries energy, which makes sense because the typical Aries personality is very impulsive, always running into things "headfirst."

Second house

In Vedic astrology, the second house is the house of possessions and belongings. It is the house of finances, income, tangible possessions, and investments. The act of using objects you own, such as cars, to their best and fullest extent is also associated with the second house.

The second house rules the neck, including the voice and vocal chords. Some Vedic astrologers include facial features, like the eyes, nose, teeth, and tongue, as some of the second house's body parts, while others associate them with the first house since it rules the head.

If your second house is strong, you may have a persuasive and delightful tone of voice, a singing talent, or skills as a public speaker. You may be excellent at sales because you can assure and manipulate others with your smooth tongue. A weak second house could indicate potential health problems in the ears, nose, and throat, or an unpleasant speaking or singing voice.

The Taurus zodiac sign is affiliated with the second house, which makes sense because Taurus individuals are often stubborn and unyielding. Their necks cannot be turned to see a different point of view once they have set their minds.

Third house

The third house relates to the intellect and memory as well as communication skills. This house governs journeys, short trips, siblings, neighbors, and intellectual pursuits. The third house is associated with all the various forms of communication, including social media, the news, phones, radios, televisions, journalism, writing, public speaking, and more. Any professions related to communication, such as public relations, marketing, motivational speaking, writing, etc., correlate with the third house.

The third house rules most of the body parts that come in pairs, such as the lungs, hands, arms, shoulders, collar bones, and legs. It also governs the nervous system. A strong third house predicts that you will be a skilled communicator or have strong lungs, hands, and arms. A weak third house could manifest as poor communication skills, anxiety, asthma, shoulder pain, broken collar bones, or weak arms and legs.

Gemini is the astrological sign associated with the third house, which makes sense because Gemini is one of the most social, communicative, and talkative signs of the zodiac.

Fourth house

The fourth house governs the home, roots, land, real estate, motherhood, maternal instincts, and the relationship with the mother. This house is very important because it predicts the domestic happiness of an individual. Careers associated with the fourth are childcare, real estate agent, or home decorator.

The body parts that correlate with the fourth house are the breasts, stomach, and digestive system. This means that a strong fourth house indicates full breasts and a balanced metabolism. A weak fourth house could signal breast cancer, digestive problems, or a weak or overactive metabolism.

The fourth house is associated with the zodiac sign Cancer, which makes sense because it is the sign symbolized by the crab, who is so closely attached to his home that he carries it on his back at all times.

Fifth house

The fifth house in Vedic astrology rules joy, pleasure, playfulness, creativity, and romance. It is associated with one's ability to experience joy or pleasure and to express oneself creatively.

This house rules over the heart, back, lower stomach, spine, and pancreas. If you have a weak fifth house, you may suffer from heart or back problems, stomach acid issues, gallbladder problems, or spinal cord disorders. A strong fifth house indicates a healthy heart and a strong back.

Although this is not directly the house of love, the association with the heart connects this sign to romantic love. A strong fifth house can indicate easy, successful romantic relationships, while a weak fifth house can signal trouble following one's heart or difficulty making and maintaining romantic connections.

This house is connected to the zodiac sign Leo, which makes sense because, as one of the most courageous and romantic signs, Leos are known for having a big, brave heart.

Sixth house

The sixth house correlates with physical health, wellness, and daily routines. While your body is ruled by the first house, the way you take care of your body and the daily habits that affect your wellness are ruled by the sixth house. This house is also related to obstacles, problems, difficulties, enemies, and unpaid debts.

A strong sixth house means it can be nearly impossible to defeat you. While it doesn't mean that your life will lack enemies and obstacles, a strong sixth house indicates that you will always vanquish your enemies and conquer obstacles that stand in your path. It also signals a strong body, attention to wellness, and mindful daily habits to care for the body, such as a healthy diet and exercise regimen.

This house rules the kidneys, intestines, and appendix. A strong sixth house indicates health in these body parts, while a weak sixth house could signal kidney stones, appendicitis, hernias, and constipation.

The sixth house relates to the Virgo astrology sign, which is easy to remember because Virgo is the sign of the virgin, an intact and healthy physical being that treats her body like a temple. Some Vedic astrologers may also associate this house with the Libra star sign.

Seventh house

The seventh house sits in opposition to the first house, which helps explain its meaning. While the first house is the house of the self and individuals, the seventh house rules couples and partnerships. The seventh house signifies marriage, relationships, contracts, business deals, and business partnerships.

The seventh house is connected to the ovaries and lower back, so a strong seventh house indicates health in these areas while a weak seventh house could predict fertility and conception issues, lower back pain, and menstrual cramps.

This house is ruled by Libra, further emphasizing the significance of romantic couples and marriages. Libra is symbolized by the two scales, representing the need for balance in any relationship or partnership.

Eighth house

The eighth house in Vedic astrology governs the length of life, death, sudden life-changing events, and near-death experiences. It governs wealth, including quick losses and gains of wealth, such as winning the lottery, inheritances, and the stock market. The eighth house also rules transformations and mysteries. The eighth house represents professions related to math, psychology, astrology, and the paranormal.

The body parts ruled by the eighth house include the pelvis and sexual organs, so issues with sexuality, reproduction, and the excretory system are related to this house. A weak eighth house can also indicate mental illnesses such as depression and anxiety.

The eighth house is governed by the zodiac sign Scorpio, which makes sense because Scorpios are all about power, and no greater power exists in the human realm than the forces of life and death.

Ninth house

The ninth house is connected to dreams, aspirations, and truth. It governs religion, long journeys, distant travel, good karma, higher education, and good luck. A strong ninth house indicates optimism and good fortune, while a weak ninth house could signify negativity and bad luck. A strong ninth house also points to frequent travel to faraway places and immigration.

This house governs the thighs, bone marrow, arteries, and the left leg. A strong ninth house predicts strong thighs and healthy blood, while a weak ninth house may predict an injury to the left leg or illness relating to the blood.

The ninth house is related to Sagittarius energy, which is easy to remember because sunny Sagittarius is the eternal optimist and the traveler of the zodiac.

Tenth house

The tenth house relates to career, profession, and reputation. A strong tenth house denotes an impressive, successful career and a good reputation, while a weak tenth house indicates career problems or a bad reputation. While the fourth house relates to maternity, the tenth house connects with the father, paternity, paternal instincts, and relationships with paternal figures, including authority figures.

The body parts that correspond with the tenth house are the knees, joints, and bones. A strong tenth house indicates health and strength in these areas, while a weak tenth house could predict arthritis, inflamed joints, bone density issues, and knee problems. Some Vedic astrologers also relate the tenth house to the skin, so issues such as acne, wrinkles, and skin allergies could be related to a weak tenth house.

This house is governed by Capricorn, which makes sense, as Capricorn is one of the hardest-working and most authoritative signs of the zodiac.

Eleventh house

The eleventh house in Vedic astrology is the house of prosperity. The eleventh house correlates with fame, fortune, and great wealth. It is also related to older siblings, friends, acquaintances, and one's social circle. It has to do with society and where one fits in the world as a whole.

The eleventh house governs the ankles, shins, and right leg. A weak eleventh house could denote weak or sprained ankles, damage to the right leg, or shin injuries. A strong eleventh house could mean powerful ankles and strong legs.

Aquarius is the ruler of the eleventh house, which is easy to remember because Aquarius is the sign of the humanitarian and cares deeply about society and close friends.

Twelfth house

As the final house in Vedic astrology, the twelfth house represents endings, the end of life and the beginning of a new life cycle, and spiritual journeys. The eighth house rules death, so the endings represented by the twelfth house have a more positive connotation. The twelfth house also rules the subconscious, so it relates to psychic abilities, secrets, dreams, energetic vibrations, and emotions.

The body parts associated with this house are the left eye, lymphatic system, and feet. A strong twelfth house indicates stability and strong feet, while a weak twelfth house can mean injuries to the left eye, orthopedic issues, and problems with the lymph nodes.

Pisces is the ruler of the twelfth house, which makes sense because Pisces is the zodiac sign most likely to possess psychic abilities.

Chapter Seven: Reading a Vedic Birth Chart (Kundli)

Once you have an understanding of the basic principles of Vedic astrology, you can combine them to read a Vedic birth chart.

A kundli or kundali is the word for a birth chart or horoscope chart in Vedic astrology. It is an astrological diagram used to predict an individual's future, personality, and purpose. To create the most accurate and complete kundli, you need your exact birth date, time, and location. You can consult an expert astrologer to create a kundli based on this information, or you can enter it into an online generator from a reputable website. The kundli is a chart that shows the planetary angles and astrological positions at the time of birth, which can then be interpreted to make predictions.

A kundli not only predicts the future but also reveals secrets of the past and present. It tells you about your physical and psychological traits, your temperament and disposition, your strengths and weaknesses, your emotional, mental, and spiritual predilections, your likes and dislikes, and your passions.

Although there are many aspects of a kundli, it is not difficult to read once you understand the significance of the houses, lunar mansions, planets, and zodiac signs. A kundli may look confusing and intimidating at first glance, but knowing the basic principles of Vedic astrology gives you everything you need to know to interpret it.

Uses of a kundli include:

- Learning how you should deal with obstacles in life, and predicting what these obstacles might be.
- Learning what opportunities may come your way, and how to make the most of them.
- Matchmaking purposes to determine your best possible match as well as predict the strengths and weaknesses of a match, what obstacles you may face as a couple, and how to overcome them.
- Discovering what career path could be the most fulfilling for you, and putting your strengths and special abilities to their best use.
- Predicting what your financial future will look like, and how you can best prepare.
- Predicting what your academic life will look like, and what type of student you will become.
- Discovering where you may have enemies, and where you can find your greatest allies.
- Predicting and explaining potential health concerns.

These are just a few of the insights you can glean from a kundli, and it is by no means a comprehensive list. You can see the importance of knowing how to read a kundli, particularly if you are a strong believer and practitioner of Vedic astrology.

How to Read Your Vedic Kundli

Here is the basic structure of a blank Vedic birth chart, before the birth information of a specific individual is applied:

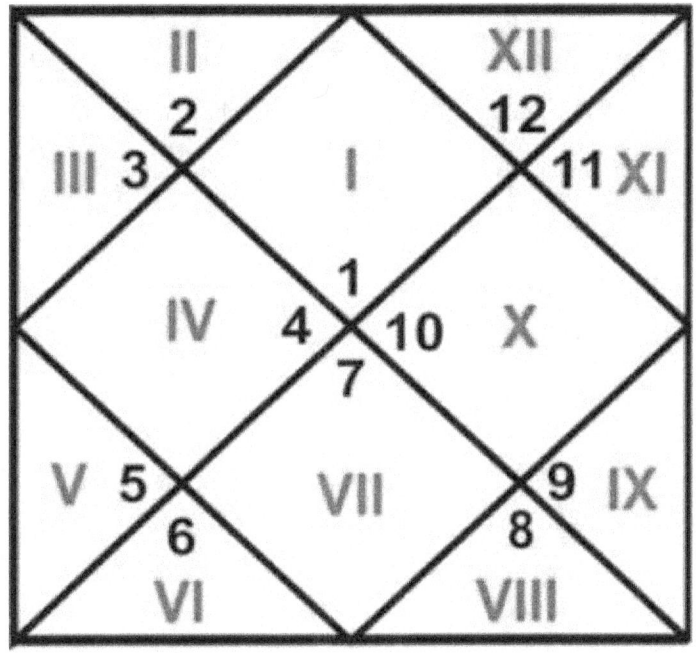

Reading this chart may seem like a daunting task, so let's break down the individual components of a kundli.

The planets in a kundli are denoted by the numerals 1-12, and the houses are denoted by Roman numerals I-XII.

The first step is to identify your Rising/Ascendant sign: on a kundli, the number in the first house represents the rising or ascendant sign. In Vedic astrology, the most important sign on the birth chart is the rising sign. The rising sign is the "mask" that you wear, the first impression you make, and the way that you appear to others. While Western astrology emphasizes the sun sign, the rising sign is considered much more important in Vedic astrology, followed by the moon sign.

The signs correlate with the numbers in this order:

1. Aries

2. Taurus

3. Gemini

4. Cancer

5. Leo

6. Virgo

7. Libra

8. Scorpio

9. Sagittarius

10. Capricorn

11. Aquarius

12. Pisces

On this chart, we can see that the Rising/Ascendant sign is Aries, positioned in the first house.

The next step is to look at the houses on the kundli. There are 12 houses with unique meanings assigned to each, and together, they tell us about your physical traits and personality characteristics.

The Roman numerals on a kundli represent the house numbers, and the significance of the houses are as follows:

First House: identity, self, physical features, body, characteristics, personality
Second House: wealth, income, finances, family values
Third House: communication, trade, hobbies, interests, intellectual pursuits, younger siblings
Fourth House: mother, home, land, property, vehicle
Fifth House: romance, love, affairs, relationships, progeny, past life experience
Sixth House: physical health, wellness, diseases, debt, enemies
Seventh House: marriage, spouse, long-term partnerships and relationships,
Eighth House: longevity, unexpected incidents, transformative events
Ninth House: higher education, luck, good karma, mentor, religion, long-distance travel
Tenth House: career, karma, father
Eleventh House: goals, place in society, good fortune, elder siblings
Twelfth House: energy, effort

Once you can recognize the houses on the chart and connect them with their associated meanings, you must find where the planets are positioned on your chart. The kundli shows exactly where the planets were positioned (in which houses) at your time of birth.

Here are the abbreviations for the planets and their meanings:

Sun (Su): source of energy and life, masculine
Moon (Mo): mind, emotions, inner or hidden self, feminine, fertility
Mercury (Me): communication, intellect, technology
Mars (Ma): courage, passion, physical strength, risk-taking, short-tempered, argumentative, anger, younger siblings
Venus (Ve): worldly pleasure, luxury, love, romance, beauty, marriage, friendship, art, music
Jupiter (Ju): spirituality, higher education, research, good luck, travel
Saturn (Sa): property, bad luck, hard work, sorrow, reputation, fame
Rahu (Ra): foreigners, international travel
Ketu (Ke): spirituality, superstitions, beliefs

And here is another chart that includes the abbreviations of the planets, so you can see what a kundli looks like with the planets and houses:

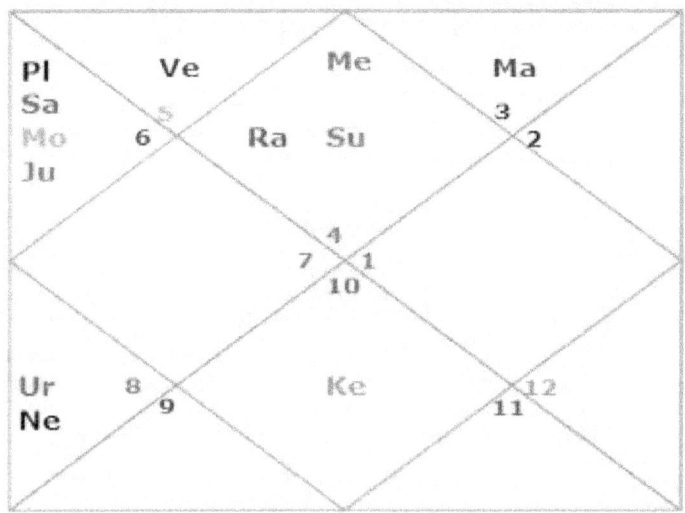

Combining this information can tell you which planets and zodiac signs are in which houses, and you can interpret it by combining the various meanings from the tables above.

Going deeper into interpreting charts by including transits (Gocharas), planetary combinations (yoga), and aspects (dristis), is the work of an experienced Vedic astrologer, but you can glean the basic information just by knowing the fundamentals described above.

Conclusion

If you have read everything in this book up to this point, then congratulations! You are an expert in the basics of Vedic astrology, and you are now equipped with all the tools and information you need to unlock the mysteries of the stars.

You now know the historical background and significance of Vedic astrology and how it differs from Western astrology. You have found answers as to why certain patterns keep appearing in your life and why some people are just born charmed and lucky while others experience more struggles and difficulties.

According to Vedic astrology, everything that happens in your life and all of your character traits are determined by the exact placement of the planets and stars at the moment of your birth. Now you can join the countless people who have been using Vedic astrology since ancient times to predict personalities, careers, relationships, and more. You can apply this information to your own life, and to the lives of your family and friends (as long as they are willing to give you their exact date, time, and location of birth!).

Now that you have learned the basic concepts of Vedic astrology, hopefully you have gained a better understanding of why you are the way you are in the present, why you have had the experiences of your past, and what you are destined for in the future. You can recognize your personal strengths and weaknesses, and maybe let go of what no longer serves you to make room for greater things to come.

You can use the tools you have learned about Vedic astrology to help you form new romantic relationships and friendships, improve your career and finances, boost your physical and mental health, and derive more joy from everyday life. The more you open up your mind, develop your intuition, and practice the concepts of Vedic astrology, the more you will be able to understand the deeper meaning of your life and find your purpose.

Vedic astrology tells us that your destiny was written in the stars at your time of birth, and it even led you to *now*, this exact moment, of finishing this text. Congratulations on starting your journey to understanding the secrets of the universe and unlocking your full potential!

www.ingramcontent.com/pod-product-compliance
Lightning Source LLC
Chambersburg PA
CBHW071504070526
44578CB00001B/435